DISCARD

Reading American History

The Star Spangled Banner

Written by Melinda Lilly
Illustrated by Yohanis Díaz

Educational Consultants
Kimberly Weiner, Ed.D
Betty Carter, Ed.D

Rourke
Publishing LLC
Vero Beach, Florida 32963

© 2003 Rourke Publishing LLC

All rights reserved. No part of this book may be reproduced or utilized in any form or by any means, electronic, or mechanical including photocopying, recording, or by any information storage and retrieval system without permission in writing from the publisher.

www.rourkepublishing.com

Gracias a la Historia, por permitirnos ser parte de ella.
Thanks to History, for allowing us to be part of her.
—Y. D.

Designer: Elizabeth J. Bender

Art Direction: Rigo Aguirre, www.versalgroup.com

Library of Congress Cataloging-in-Publication Data

Lilly, Melinda.
 The Star spangled banner / Melinda Lilly; illustrated by Yohanis Díaz.
   p. cm. — (Reading American history)
 Summary: A simple description of how, during the War of 1812, Francis Scott Key came to write the poem that became the national anthem.
  ISBN 1-58952-365-2
  1. Baltimore, Battle of, 1814—Juvenile literature. 2. United States—History—War of 1812—Flags—Juvenile literature. 3. Flags—United States—History—19th century—Juvenile literature. 4. Star-spangled banner (Song)—Juvenile literature. [1. Flags—United States. 2. Key, Francis Scott, 1779-1843. 3. Star-spangled banner (Song) 4. United States—History—War of 1812.] I. Díaz, illus. II. Title.

E356.B2 L45 2002
782.42'1599'0973—dc21   2002017846

Cover Illustration: Francis Scott Key looks at the Star Spangled Banner.

Printed in the USA

Time Line

Help students follow this story by introducing important events in the Time Line.

1812 U. S. declares war on Britain in what is later called the War of 1812.

1813 The Star Spangled Banner is sewn by Mary Young Pickersgill and others, including her 13-year-old daughter Caroline.

1814 Washington, D. C. is burned by British soldiers.

1814 Francis Scott Key writes the "Star Spangled Banner," after the Battle of Baltimore.

1815 The War of 1812 ends.

1931 The "Star Spangled Banner" becomes the U. S. national anthem.

The **Star Spangled Banner** is **America**'s song.

It is also a name for our flag!

Singing America's song

The flag flew when America and **England** were at war in 1814. American **Francis Scott Key** saw it flying at **Fort McHenry**.

Francis Scott Key sees the flag.

English ships saw the flag, too.

The ships aimed **cannons** at the fort.

English ships aim at Fort McHenry.

All day and night cannons fired.
War filled the sky.

The English fire cannons at the fort.

By morning, the fight was over.

The next morning

Francis Scott Key tried to see the Star Spangled Banner.
If it flew, America had won the fight.

Francis Scott Key looks at the fort.

He saw the flag at the fort.
America had won the fight!

The flag at Fort McHenry

Key wrote a **poem** about the flag.

Key writes.

That poem is now our **national anthem**, the "Star Spangled Banner."

Looking at the old flag and the poem

Word List

America (uh MER ih kuh)—The United States

cannons (KAN unz)—Mounted guns

England (ING glund)—Part of the country of Great Britain and the United Kingdom

Fort McHenry (FORT muk HEN ree)—The fort at Baltimore harbor

Key, Francis Scott (KEE, FRAN sis SKOT)—Author of the "Star Spangled Banner," Francis Scott Key was also a lawyer.

national anthem (NASH uh nul AN thum)—The song of the U. S.

poem (POH em)—Written verse

Star Spangled Banner (STAR SPANG guld BAN er)—The flag and song of the U. S.; the flag that flew at Fort McHenry during the Battle of Baltimore

Books to Read

Bateman, Teresa. *Red, White, Blue and Uncle Who?: The Story Behind Some of America's Patriotic Symbols.* Holiday House, 2001.

Kroll, Steven. *By the Dawn's Early Light: The Story of the Star-Spangled Banner*. Scholastic, 2000.

Quiri, Patricia Ryon. *The National Anthem*. Children's Press, 1998.

Ryan, Pam Munoz. *The Flag We Love*. Charlesbridge Publishing, 2000.

Websites to Visit

www.nps.gov/fomc/tguide/Contents.htm

www.bcpl.net/~etowner/patriots.html

www.loc.gov/exhibits/treasures/trm065.html

www.usflag.org/francis.scott.key.html

http://web8.si.edu/nmah/htdocs/ssb-old/2_home/fs2.html

Index

America 5, 6, 15, 17, 22

England 6, 22

Fort McHenry 6, 9, 17, 22

Key, Francis Scott 3, 6, 15, 19, 22

Star Spangled Banner 3, 5, 15, 20, 21, 22